DON'T STAND UNDER A FLOCK OF ANGRY BIRDS!

MIKE G. WILLIAMS

ISBN: 1494292254
ISBN-13: 978-1494292256

Other Books by Mike G. Williams

Turkey Soup For The Sarcastic Soul Vol 1

Turkey Soup For The Sarcastic Soul Vol 2

Life Happens: Shut Up, Smile, and Carry a Plunger

An Amateur's Guide To Skunk Repair

*Men Moved To Mars When Women Started
Killing The Ones On Venus*

Love Is Not A Three Letter Word

Disclaimer:

Mike G. Williams is not associated in any way with the creators, producers, builders, designers, owners, authors, or legal representatives of the wonderful, amazing Rovio Entertainment Ltd. This book is not meant to be derogatory, in any way, to the above aforementioned organization. This book would not have been possible without the incredible insight and wisdom written into every Angry Birds app. The author wishes to thank Rovio Entertainment Ltd. for the creation and production of Angry Birds as a wonderful teaching tool for today's young person. May the odds be ever in their favor.

DEDICATION

To my children, who taught me how to play Angry Birds and allowed me to play it with them. To the children of the electronic generation everywhere, may you somehow find insight into living through the games you play and the examples my generation has left for you (or in some cases failed to leave for you). Seek the wisdom that is truly all around you. There are great lessons in everything you see and experience if you look hard enough. Some of the lessons are easy to learn and some are not. Always remember that wisdom's reward is a great life.

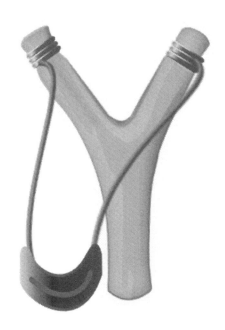

CONTENTS

FORWARD

I occupy almost two-hundred different airplane seats every year, more than many pilots. I am simply the guy in seat 6A with the Bose headphones draped over his fleshy looking cranium and the computer on his tray table steaming with ideas. I usually use the flying time to write, but occasionally to catch up on my beauty sleep. If you have seen my less than spectacular facial appearance, you can tell I have spent more time in writing than in beauty sleeping. For many around me, flying is a time to get their game on.

It was mid-May and my family and I were again headed to spend the summer in the Dominican Republic building water purification systems for poor villages. I will not clutter this book with the reasoning for that. I was elected to take the middle seat, which is fine for me, I rest or work equally well in any seat. On my left sat Coleman, my nine year old son, and on my right sat Careagan my seven year old daughter. They were as quiet as mice as they sat feverishly tapping the screens of their latest handheld devices. The silence was broken by an occasional outburst of exuberance or despair. Today, and for the past week their game of choice has been Angry Birds Space. At the time I did not know which version of the game it was. To be honest, at the time I didn't even know there were more than one.

I watched as my son and daughter helped each other destroy the embedded, evil, pigs from their makeshift bunkers and obstacles. I watched them squeal with joy upon the destruction of the pigs. I remember wondering

1

if PETA (People For The Ethical Treatment of Animals) or the humane Society has given this game their seal of approval. I wasn't judging, I just wondered. It was somewhere during this flight that my children asked me to play the game with them. Well ... kind of play with them. I was to take control when they could not get past a level and try to help them. It felt good to be asked for help. As a parent, I was made for this. I will most likely lose this ability when they are teenagers. Any parent reading this knows what I mean.

It was in the midst of that game that I came to learn that life lessons can be gleaned in the strangest of places. Here, for one dollar and ninety-nine cents was some wisdom for me and my children that mirrored that of Solomon the Great. With this statement some of you will immediately label me as a heretic. To you I apologize and ask you to give me some humorous levity. I would never question the superior wisdom of a great leader who had over one thousand wives ... but I digress. So maybe it will choose to simply mirror the wisdom of Dr. Who.

It was on that little flight with the Angry Birds game that I was reminded of all the basic principles of success in life. Later that day my children taught me about UnBlock Me, and Fruit Ninja. All of which I found to be fascinatingly motivational and encouraging. This book is my attempt to bring to light the wisdom of those supposedly angry little flying fowl. So now without further ado ... I present to you the wisdom I learned playing Angry Birds!

Play on my friends ... and learn.
Mike G. Williams

One Blogger writes about Angry Birds:

Save the angry Angry Birds at all cost! Future survival of the Angry Birds is at stake. You must dish out revenge on the green pigs who have stolen the eggs from the birds. Use your unique destructive Angry Bird power to lay waste to the fortified hideouts of the pigs. This game features many hours of gameplay, challenging physics-based castle demolition, and much replay fun. Experience 120 levels requiring logic, skill, and brute force to crush the enemy. Save the angry Angry Birds at all cost!

 # *PLAYING TO WIN*

Nobody goes to the Olympics hoping to win fourth place...

Let's be honest, the objective of the game is the same as all other games. Win. Win, win and win again! Everyone likes winning. One wins at Angry Birds by launching various wingless (non-self-propelled) birds toward a group of smiling pigs bunkered in various shelters. You do this "bird launching" from the sling-shottish looking tree toward the enemy pigs, and thus destroying them and their fortresses. For the record, at this point in my gaming experience I have no idea why the birds have no wings and cannot fly. It is sad.

Pull back on the sling mechanism, use your finger to choose a trajectory, lift same finger, and watch the wingless wonders go sailing. Your bird goes hurling through the air on a seemingly enjoyable kamikaze mission to annihilate the pigs.

Bask in the glory of a full color HD bird-pig jihad! For what reason? We are told it is revenge. The flying bird strikes at the pillar of a bunker, or side, or top, it matters little at first. Explosions are involved to add excitement! The hope is to bring the bunker down upon the pigs thus destroying them. You are named winner when you destroy all the cowering pigs.

Winning in life is when you have been a success. That is an easy statement to make. Any motivational speaker, teacher, counselor, minister, rabbi, or bum on the street could probably tell you that. Great, but what is success? In the game of real life I might suggest that success or winning comprises of a little more than just taking out a couple of pigs in-between searching YouTube or texting you BFF.

In order that you not be disappointed later, please note that success in life is rarely marked by the latest Korean dance sensation. Success in real life is found in three areas. Firstly, your integrity. Secondly, your accomplishments. Finally, the joy of the journey. Let me ask a series of questions that I believe have self- evident answers to each of these three.

Integrity: Do you do things the right way, or the wrong way? Are you cheating your way to the top? Are you stepping on others on your way up? Are you losing your family or friends in getting to the winners circle? When you finish the race will people say, 'goodbye" or "good riddance"? Do people call you, "true to your word"? Are you honest? Are you the same person when people are watching you as you are in the darkness of a secret place? Are you a person of openness or a person of secrets?

Accomplishment: Are you genuinely doing anything of value each day? On your present path, continuing your current lifestyle and activities, what do you plan to give back to the planet from which you took years of oxygen from? Does your life say, "Thank you" or "I want it all"? Considering all that the country within which you were born has provided you, what have you given to others? If you live seventy years, will you have produced seventy years' worth of good for this world, for your family, for your friends, for those whom you have never met? Those with lofty ambitions might ask, "Am I changing the world for the better because of my life?"

Have you ever defined your own personal purpose in life? What do you believe you are here for? What would you like to accomplish if you knew you could do it? Solve the world water crisis? Feed the planet? Stop global warming? Make McDonald's food healthy? Stop global cooling? Invent a tasty seedless watermelon? Cure cancer? Invent additional flavors of Hot Pockets? Anything?

Joy in the journey: Are you enjoying the years of your life or enduring them? Do you find peace in your heart with each decision you make? Do you lay your head down at night proud of the work you have accomplished? Will the continuation of your present path lead you to a place of happy endings or of angry endings? Do you experience contentment in your life? Do you experience excitement in your life? Do people note you as a smiler or a frowner? Is your glass half full or half empty or half empty with dirty water and a cracked rim?

Someone once said, "Winning isn't everything, it is the only thing." To that I agree if you understand that winning is more than just procuring a gold medal. Actual winning is receiving the gold medal without scandal. It is doing it in a manner that does not require you to return your gold medal in years to come. It is doing it in a way that allows you to look your opponent in the face without malice or deceit. So yes ... winning with integrity, accomplishment, and joy should be the goal in the game of life.

On a side note. One bumper sticker stated, "He who dies with the most toys wins." Another read, "He who dies with the most toys is still dead."

Sum It Up

Winning in life will be determined somewhere in the contemplative years of your retirement. The moments that you will reflect on and judge as to whether or not you did anything of value with the time you had been given to live. A great man of wisdom once said, "Winning could be simply defined as achieving what you set out to achieve, but true winning is also being happy with what you achieved!" Make sure you win at the game of life.

One Word: **Win**

Action Point

Make a list of what you would describe as successful achievements in the life of a true winner. Describe why you admire them.

#2 THAT'S EASY

Let's be honest, looks can be deceiving...

When I first looked at those two brilliant children of mine tapping away at Angry Birds I marveled to myself at how easy it looked. As I sat watching them struggle to complete a level, I pondered at just how easily I could have done that ... without even looking. It was not until my daughter asked me to help her conquer a level, that I realized how tough firing birds at pigs could be. She explained what to do and I let the birds fly with pride knowing that I would certainly enjoy a pig roast in no time.

After my twentieth attempt at that particular round, I finally scored a win! It was harder than it looked. I learned that just because I had "mastered" one puzzle did not mean that the next one was going to be that much easier. Sure, I had learned some necessary principles, but each puzzle and level brought with it the need to remember past lessons, and incorporate the new lessons I would need to learn.

As I have come to be older I have found life to be the same way. Every day I compete to destroy my enemies. The enemies I am trying to destroy are not people or embedded pigs, rather I fight a battle every day with apathy, mediocrity, and decreasing energy. Apathy is that lazy streak that is in all of us from time to time. Mediocrity, the willingness to settle for less than the best.

The temptation to slack off is always there, and even greater now that I have less energy. I have to confess that as a father, life has not become any easier. In fact, it may be getting harder.

I sat on an airplane with a Rubik's Cube master last year. Rubik's Cubes were the handheld game of my generation. There was no Rubik's Cube Rio or Rubik's Cube Space either. One game, play it or sit there and twiddle your thumbs. Don't laugh. The little cubes are harder than they look. This guy sat there for the entire flight from Tampa to Los Angeles fiddling with the multicolored cube. He would close his eyes, and twist and turn it every which way. He would toss it up, catch it and twist some more to keep his mind from subconsciously remembering the way to bring it back to correct.

I could not resist striking up a conversation with this guy. It turns out that he was no bone-head! He was working on an advanced degree at a very prestigious university. He explained that he was in the top ten in the world in solving the cube. He handed me the cube and asked me to mess up the order. He looked it over, closed his eyes, began twisting, eyes still closed, solving it from memory alone in about five-seconds. Yes, with his eyes closed the whole time! Wow! I asked him what the secret was. Certainly there has to be a secret, or a short cut, or a hidden magical trick. *Where is the magic wand? "Dude, that was Voodoo!"* No. It was just plain practice. He told me that every second of his time his hand was solving the multicolored puzzle. I asked him if he slept with it. He said, "I have never intentionally slept with it, but I do wake up with it still in my hands most mornings."

In his book entitled The Outliers, Malcomb Gladwell presents an interesting case for those, one would call "extremely successful". Gladwell repeatedly touts what he calls the "10,000 hour rule". He claims the key to success in any field is, to a large extent, a matter of practicing a specific task for a total of around 10,000 hours.

If he is correct, this means you can be the next LeBron James, Kobe Bryant or Michael Jordon (of my generation) in only 10,000 hours of dedication to the sport of basketball.

The game of life looks easy from a distance. A successful life is one that is strategically lived. Living with integrity, accomplishment, and joy must be done strategically. It must be planned, practiced and re-practiced. Your desired occupation must be planned, practiced and re-practiced. Life is not for slackers. It was never meant to be. Whatever you desire, be it a skill or a quality, will take hours of work. But you can do it. Yes you can!

Sum It Up

Anything worth doing is going to take hard work. Even if you are naturally talented at something, remember there are others just as naturally talented as you. You must develop that natural talent and turn it from good to great. The difference between Michael Jordon and Michael Gordon is work! *Who is Michael Gordon? We don't know, I guess he didn't practice 10,000 hours. That is a shame. I'll bet he would have been great.*

One Word: *Effort*

Action Point

What do you have a natural talent for? What will it take for you to go from average to awesome? You must decide whether you want to be a superstar or not, and if you are willing to pay the price!

#3 YOU HAVE WHAT IT TAKES

Let's get off the negativity train...

So there I sat, working on the next pig battle. Yep, there I sat working on it for another twenty-five attempts. There were times when I thought it was unsolvable. I remember telling my son that it would be a lot easier if they would let me choose the type of birds I could use. I would pick the huge powerhouse birds every time. Alas, I did not get a choice. However, with perseverance I came to the realization that each round could be completed effectively and victoriously with the birds I had been given. That is good news. You might think that you will never solve one particular problem, but if you work long enough and hard enough, you will.

Now after the last chapter you might have a big question. You might be secretly asking yourself, "Do I really have what it takes to be a winner?" I have a big answer. "YES! Yes you do." You are not a complete cosmic anomaly. You are not totally different from everybody else. You may have a little less brain power than some, but you also have a lot more than others who have succeeded. You may have a little less natural talent than some, but you also have a lot more talent than others. There will always be someone who has more of something than you do, but know that there will always be someone who has less.

I know that most of you reading this book are living here in North America. You were born in the land of unique opportunity. You were born in the land of "Yes You Can!" You were born, or at least brought here to the place that helps losers win. You have what it takes. Let's be honest, the greatest achievers throughout history have come from the humblest of beginnings.

Now, secretly, deep down inside some of us is an angry little lying pig of doubt. That pig wants to depress you. That pig wants you to think that somehow you lack what it takes. Some of you have been lied to by someone who was supposed to have told you the truth. They failed. Those who are failing in life often want to bring those around them down to their level. Do not listen to them. These are not the people who cause the universe to continue, these are those who cause the cosmos to puke.

Listen to me. You, deep down inside you, the real you, have what it takes to be a success. You can achieve more than you think. You can accomplish more than you think. I believe it was Zig Ziglar who said, "I choose to have strong days instead of weekdays, and strong ends instead of weekends." I know that he stretched the homonyms, but his statement brings a lot of truth to our retina display.

Choose now to reject the little lying pigs that tell you that you could never top any level you have reached, because you can. That is the way the game was made to be. You have been given everything you need in order to win. Go for it. Never doubt! You can accomplish your dreams and goals. Be empowered. Be response-able! Bask in your innate capability.

Sum It Up

You don't need what everybody else has, you need to use what you have to the fullest extent. That WILL be enough for great success.

One Word: *Capable*

Action Point

Make a little list of things in which you have come to believe that you will never succeed in. Now go to a safe place and set that list on fire. Then stomp on the ashes. That list was a lie.

#4 LEARN TO ADAPT- LIFE ISN'T FAIR

We don't always get the same birds— deal with it...

In the last round I tried to clearly articulate to you the profound truth that everything you need for success is right there inside of you. You have what it takes. You are capable! Now I am going to expound on that by saying something that may seem negative. You may have noticed that not every bird being flung from our slingshots have the same strength. They don't all have the same explosive trick. Some are fast. Some are slow. Some you may think would be better to not have at all. The truth is that we don't all receive the same talents. We don't have equal physical resources. We don't have equal brain power. We and our circumstances are all completely different.

Let's talk brain power for a minute. Some of you reading this book have that. Some are as the age old adage declares, "a wise old bird". *Some of you have a very high IQ and have scored phenomenally on SATs, others would have to use a spell checker to assure themselves that they spelled phenomenally, phenomenally well.* Some of you might be MENSA level, while others are thinking "who's MENSA?". Here is the good news and bad news all in one shot. Are you ready? Not everyone receives the same *leg up* in life as the person next to them. However, in spite of that, know that you can attain a good level ... if you really want it.

What I am about to say is not one of those self-deprecating, obligatory statements. I am merely being truthful. I am no rocket scientist. The most used function on my computer is the spell check feature. There are more red and green dashed lines on the first draft of my papers than there are on a stock market crash report. I was not a naturally gifted child, I went to special classes to learn to read. I really should not be writing a book, or in my case multiple books. I cannot type very well, I still type with four fingers. Yes, this entire manuscript, my six previous books, and all those that were never published and still hiding in my book folder were all typed using just four fingers and my right thumb on the space bar. It was not until this summer that I learned that the "&" symbol was known formally as an ampersand. I learned that from listening to a comedian make jokes about it. I say all this to prove that I am unequivocally qualified to inform you that although you don't always get the same leg up as the person next to you, you can often reach the same heights as them if you really want it bad enough. You may even surpass them. Desire often triumphs over privilege. Necessity is the mother of invention! *On a side note, nobody has ever listed who the father of invention was. Maybe that explains to me why necessity seemed to disappear for a few months back in her high school days.*

I am told that the great physicist, Albert Einstein believed that he only used about 10% of his brain capacity. The average person is said to use only about 6% of their brain capacity. Translate that to mean that the average man is using 40% less brain power than the great Albert Einstein. That is great news! That means that you and I are only 40% below genius! Ergo, we have even more potential for growth than the great scientist. *Especially since he has no more potential at this point in his late life.* Again, you don't always get the same leg up as the person next to you receives, however you can still reach the same height as they can if you really want it bad enough.

Phenomenal success comes from the most unexpected places. Oddly enough, it seems that those who were faced with the greatest obstacles have been those who rose to the greatest heights. Your world is filled with negativity and naysayers, let their voices fall on deaf ears. You can be a success. You can be a winner. The fact that you don't start at the top assures you that you have a greater chance for enormous success.

This is not positive thinking mumbo-jumbo! This is truth. You will have shortcomings, we all do, it makes us human. Mine is language skills. Nevertheless, I have learned to use what I have to the best of my abilities, and I bet that you can too. There are those who chose to blame their own failures on the unfairness of life. Those people rarely achieve success. Choose to see your shortcomings as obstacles that can be overcome if you try hard enough.

Sum It Up

I have read enough autobiographies to know that most of the "World Changers" did not come from wealth, or power. The "World Changers" came from the most humble of beginnings. These men and women learned to take the adversities which came against them and turn them around for the good of themselves and mankind. As the famous writer of "The Eagle Song" once said, "Take that which is coming against you, turn it around, and use it to lift you up higher. The hurdler views the hurdles as part of the race and not as an unfair hindrance to victory.

One Word: *Adapt*

Action Point

What do you feel is a personal obstacle in your life? Now what can you do to destroy that obstacle with the birds you have been given?

#5 A LITTLE HELP FROM MY FRIENDS

Don't be ashamed to ask for help...

I owned a slingshot when I was a kid. mine was an aluminum model with a wrist strap. I was pretty good at it. We were not launching birds but rather launching little rocks or steel ball bearings and our target of choice was windows. I can still feel the rush associated with the amazing sound of breaking glass. To this day it brings tears of joy to my eyes. But after playing my first few rounds of Angry Birds I found myself unable to destroy the pig bunkers and pass the level. I tried repeatedly. My son leaned over and explained that some birds can explode with great destructive force into multiple birds causing greater bunker damage. I could do this by tapping the bird on the head while in flight. *I informed them that he would achieve the same effect with his Mother. Needless to say, they didn't get the joke.*

Soon I was launching birds, and using their special skills to take out the enemy with precision and valor. I felt as If I possessed awesome sharpshooter skills, but I never would have beaten that early level if had not let my son give me the much needed instruction. Yes, The child who was over forty years my junior gave me critical information. This was knowledge I needed if I was to win.

Sometimes our own pride will keep us from asking for help. Sometimes within our ego and psyche are these little pig voices that attempt to convince us that asking for help is a sign of weakness. These voices are liars! In fact, not asking for help is a greater sign of weakness. It might even be a sign of mental illness! Many people go through life trying to make it on their own. They never listen to anyone. *These people are known mostly by their epithet - idiot.* Everyone needs to have a team behind them. My grandfather used to have a goat. A big old billy goat called Buster. Whereas Buster was big enough to knock a grown man down to the ground he looked very friendly. He had that billy goat smile, you know the one, the one that says, "Open the door to the pen sweet child and climb on in here with me ... we'll have fun.", that kind of smile. Grandpa informed me that Buster would butt me with his double horned head if I got in that pen. Nonetheless he looked so friendly, so utterly adorable. He would eat out of my hand through the fence, certainly he would not attempt to harm me! I bet you can tell what happened next. Yes, one day I unlatched the two hasps on the door and entered the goat cage. I remember the billy goat looking at me. It was those same eyes, but now they were giving mixed messages. Now those eyes were saying, "Hello child, welcome to my world. I have some delicious Turkish Delight candy over here a little farther into my pen." Now those eyes were saying, "Did I take six shots or only five...are you feeling lucky punk!" Surely enough, Buster, good old kind Buster, "let me eat out of your hand Buster", "wouldn't hurt a fly Buster"; was now chasing me around the pen trying to run me through with his blunt boney head.

Grandpa taught me a lot of things before he took his last breath. Some I remember, some I don't, although I wish I could remember them all. He taught me that if you walk behind a donkey it could kick you. After learning the old man was right about the goat, I simply took his word on the donkey. Those donkey legs seem like they might be able to pack a punch!

Asking for help. Asking for advice. Seeking guidance. Reading the instructions. All of those are good things. We don't use GPS to prove that we are going the way we hoped we were going. We use it to get us moving in the right direction and to keep us in the right direction. I have learned that the fastest way to success is by reading, and re-reading the directions. If I am going to build a house, I am going to look at the plans over and over again until I fully understand the process for completing the house. Good direction often comes from others and becomes a team for you.

I am not a tree person. I never studied them in school. I have never read a book about them. But I did read an article about the Sequoia Trees that caught my interest. These trees grow to an incredible height. Hundreds of feet at times. What makes their height so incredible is the fact that their root system is so small in comparison to their height. By themselves their root system would not handle the great weight and width of their branches or the wind trying to topple their height. However, when they cluster together, when they link arms (well roots), they become a super-rooting system for each other. Together they are greater than the sum of their parts. They become a team for each other. They have to accept the help from others to achieve their individual greatness.

Sum It Up
It is not wrong to have friends. Having genuine friends is a great thing. People who can work in cooperative teamwork with others will experience a lift and creativity of the group which is greater than their individual abilities.

One Word: *Teamwork*

Action Point
Who are you surrounding yourself with? Are these people who will lift you up or bring you down? Are they encouragers or discouragers? Who do you need to cut from the root team roster? Who do you need to add? Make a list.

#6 BE INQUISITIVENESS AND BEYOND

Ask some good questions on your journey...

The Ostrich, as far as I know is not one of the birds in our angry little game. Maybe when we get to "Angry Birds - The Great African Savanna", we will get to launch them. *Do you think they will do an Angry Birds Savanna Edition? That would be cool.* For many years the Ostrich had a negative rap. This negative rap was truthfully just an old myth. Nevertheless the myth stood for many years. The myth said the Ostrich would bury his head in the sand when danger approached. Let me again proclaim that this so-called Ostrich fact has been debunked, but the saying has stayed.

As my journey in bird-pig warfare progressed to Angry Birds Space, things got a little more intense. We were nearing the end of our flight and my son was making noises that sounded like he had become a bitter angry beleaguered pig. He blurted, "It won't go where I'm launching it... the bird flies where it's not supposed to." Looking over and watching him play, I quickly realized that his primary school education had not yet fully covered the effects of gravity on the trajectory of virtual birds entering a virtual planet's virtual gravitational pull. I was able to point out to him the effects of gravity, and how to take that into account when you are hurling birds at pigs. *It also comes in real handy if you ever want to work for NASA and not be pink slipped on the first week of rocket launching when you miss the moon and land in Area 51. I can almost hear Donald Trump saying, "You're fired!"*

Some of you might think that this chapter is another about asking for help. Wrong! This lesson is giving you the right to ask the tough questions. Even if those questions stand up in the face of conventional wisdom or traditional ways of doing things. Stay with me for a minute.

Success in the struggles of everyday life is not about positive thinking, or even holding out hope for a miracle. A positive attitude will help, but it will not be the be all and end all. Some people place much emphasis on positive thinking. I love those people. Good for them, "You go boy. You go girl." Nevertheless, I want to re-direct emotions for a minute. Faced with any problem, you can move forward with a multitude of responses. We all have options. You can just think happy thoughts and hope the problem works itself out. You can worry and fret over the problem. You can yell at the problem and blame those whom you think caused it. You can grumble that life is rigged to bring these problems your way. Or ... (drum roll please) you can sit down and take a look at the problem from all sides and probe deeply for an answer. Look, if you are going to see genuine solutions to whatever your problem is, eventually someone is going to have to ask the right questions. Why can it not be you? Why should it not be you? Who has a more vested interest in your problem and future success than you?

So next time you are faced with a real life dilemma, an actual problem, a genuine injustice, or stubborn incongruity in your life, sit down and take out a note pad. Identify the problems. Write them down. There is usually always more than one when you really get down to the root. Ask questions that allow you to find out the genuine source of the problem.

My son, in his youthful impatience, thought the game was messed up and out to get him. The truth was that he had three problems. Firstly, he had not the foggiest understanding of gravity. Secondly, he had never counted on the fact that mathematics was going to come into play in an

Angry Birds game. Thirdly, the full problem was not a rigged game at all but actually an uninformed player. Him!

I like questions. So here we go. What problems have you faced in the past week? How about the past month or even the past year? How did you handle them? Did you go all "Ostrich" on it? Did you bury your head in the sand. Those who win in life are not those who bury their heads. They are not those who blame their problems on the system! They are not those who claim their problems are the fault of everything and everyone around them. Winners stop and look at the problem from every angle. They are willing to identify the genuine foundational problems that are the root of the scenario they are facing. Winners can even see when they are part of that foundational mix of problems. Winners then systematically begin working on the foundational problem in order to eliminate the surface problem.

What if you didn't have to wait for a problem to ask a question? What if you could look at the good, praise it, and then go on to ask what it would take to make the good better? Could you then ask questions to make the better great? Could you then ask and answer questions to make the great become phenomenal? Iconoclastic? Legendary? Questions are the best friend of progress and repeated success. *Ask the Apple Man himself, Steve Jobs, if he would agree with this point. Well, if you could, you understand.*

Sum It Up

When faced with a problem don't run from it. Don't put it off. Look at it from all angles. Get some other people to help you identify the root cause (and most often causes) of your problem. Then you can decide the best way to handle your problem. In everything you do in the future or are doing, be inquisitive. Don't settle for the way it is, ask the questions that cause improvement if nothing else. The great songwriter said, "Never write a song that does not answer a question." Ask questions.

One Word: *Inquisitive*

Action Point

Outside of problems, what are you doing good right now? What are the hurdles you could overcome to do it better? If you're making an A in English right now, what could you do to make it an A⁺?

#7 PRIORITIZE YOUR ATTACK

Do the important stuff first...

It did not take long for me to realize that simply launching birds randomly at these bunkers was not as damaging to the pigs as I had hoped. I would knock over beams around them and crush one or two sending them into virtual piggy heaven. Somehow there was always one left to look at me with that piggish grin as if to say, "That's all you got, big shot comedy guy?" I quickly realized the there was a strategy to every bunker. Each level had an order in which to beat it. You had to take out the correct beams first.

My father often said to me, "First things first." *To which I would sarcastically respond, "And last things last - duh."* Of course I would say that only to myself. I grew up in an age where to say that out loud to a parent would have landed you in a fair bit of trouble. *Let's just say that my generation did not have "Time Outs" we had "Knock Outs!" The time out was the time you spent recovering from your knock-out ... but I digress.* Dad was trying to tell me that if I didn't do the first things first I would never even get to the second things. I would never see the third things.

Let me give an example. In front of you there is a non-virtual T-bone steak, a real one. There is a knife, a fork, A1 Steak sauce, a plate, a propane gas stove, a pan, and an empty propane tank. Unless you like your steak the way you like your sushi (aka raw) you would best (1) fill the gas tank, before you (2) heat up the pan, before you (3) cook your steak until it's 140 degrees throughout, before you (4) put it on a plate, before you (5) sit down and eat it. One quick question. What are we drinking? Are we having anything with the steak? *Are you familiar with the concept of "vegetable side dishes" or are we all Neanderthal carnivores? Side dishes are people too you know!*

Is this a chapter about cooking? No. It is a chapter about learning that if you don't complete the important stuff first, you will never get anything of importance and greatness done. I remember my professor years ago in front of the class with a glass pitcher. Into the glass pitcher he first put a big rock. It practically filled the entire pitcher. He asked us, "Is the pitcher full?" "Yes," we responded. Then he poured some medium sized fish tank gravel in around the big rock. He got in his whole bag of additional medium fish tank grave. He asked us again, "Is the pitcher full?" "Yes, now it really is!" we responded. He laughed and added an entire bag of sand into the pitcher. The small diameter of the sand allowed it to run through the big rocks and the little rocks and filled up the cracks and crevasses from the bottom to the top. He asked us, "Is the pitcher full now class?" "Yes, now it surely is," some responded. Others responded, "You wouldn't ask that if you didn't want to trick us ... so our answer is no." He then opened a can of Coca-Cola and poured it into the pitcher. The sand absorbed it all. He opened another, and another, and another. Each time the sand gulped up the liquid sugar until the entire six-pack was absorbed. *What a waste of Coca-Cola! Nevertheless it was an awesome demonstration.*

The lesson was *NOT* teaching us to do more and more and more. The lesson clearly showed that if he had not put the important things (the big rocks) in the pitcher first, he would never have been able to fit the other things into the pitcher. There is an order to life. The successful person learns to prioritize that which is important, and put their effort toward those things first. All of your life people are going to be pulling for you to do what they believe is important. It may be very important to them, but that does not mean that it is important to the goals you wish to accomplish in your life. Prioritize. Do that which is most important first. Look at where you want to be, what you want to accomplish in life, and work hard on those major goals first.

One more illustration, just because I can. *I control the keypad.* There you stand with your To Do List on your iPhone. It is long. There are twenty-five items on the list. Important stuff like Finish an online course in Spanish, apply for a new job, download fourteen free apps you want to try, get groceries, and call your mother. You know you need to. You haven't talked to her since Thanksgiving, the same thanksgiving that you told your Uncle Ralph you thought his side of the family were losers. You did not say that on purpose, it was a Freudian slip. You meant to say "pass the potatoes" and it just came flying out! So you really need to call her and apologize. Then there is the need to call that perfect person you finally got a number for. You need to get on the phone before they are connected to somebody else, somebody who already has full time employment. *Free burritos or not, you can't work at Toms Taco Truck forever. As a college graduate you are way overqualified to get manager position anyway. Seriously, Tom can't even put an apostrophe to show possession in his sign name. Duh!*

Stop for just a moment and put a priority number on each of the items in the list above. Now in the midst of numbering and prioritizing the items above, imagine you notice a little toddler meandering aimlessly out onto a busy street (feel the tension in the story). In a split second you scan the horizon for the parent to come racing out to grab the child. In a split second you realize that the mother has somehow lost her train of thought while talking on her cell to the people at the home shopping network about returning an innovative designer baby bath cat litter box combination. What will you do? Your mind immediately goes into priority mode. Well, hopefully it does. The priority of the moment is to save the child. Yes, buying the new car or downloading a new game is also very important, but right now your gut tells you to put a yellow highlighter on SAVE BABY NOW! Now go save the imaginary child!

Sum It Up

We all have a To Do List. You have one even if you don't know it. Even if you don't have it written down. Inside your head, subconsciously, is a list of hopes, dreams, plans, desires, hungers, tom-foolery, and I could go on. Locate all those items and bring them to one spot in your brain. Now figure out which are the "Big Important Things" and go do them first. That is the whole lesson. Consider the truth of the other lessons in this book and decide which things are really, truly, genuinely the Big Things, the Rocks. Prioritize! Rocks first, stones second, sand next and Coca-Cola last of all.

One Word: *Prioritize*

Action Point

Make a list of the important things to you desire to accomplish with your week, your month, your year, your life. Put some numbers on them. Now put numbers on the list that represent how you have been prioritizing them. Think about it.

#8 MAKE EVERY SHOT COUNT

Not everyone can come from behind for a win...

I learned very quickly that getting off to a good start was a great key to winning at Angry Birds. All it took was miscalculating that first launch and you might as well just go back and start the level over. The precision needed to win when you wasted a bird was almost beyond recovery. Thus when you are playing you must make every bird launch count. I remember another story about a bird, not an angry one. This one was of the winged variety and did not need slingshot to get to where it had to go. *It had wings.*

Eddie Rickenbacker is a famous World War 2 aeronautical hero. On one of his flying missions across the Pacific Ocean, he and his seven-member crew went down at sea. Miraculously, all of the men survived the emergency water landing (aka crash). After climbing onto a life raft, Rickenbacker and his men floated for days on the rough waters of the Pacific, fighting the sun, fighting sharks, and most of all fighting hunger. By the eighth day their rations ran out. No food. No water. They were, as we say, a thousand miles from nowhere and nobody knew they were there. They needed more than a little luck, they needed a miracle.

It was a hot afternoon waiting, and waiting, and waiting when Rickenbacker led the men in prayers and they all prayed for a miracle. Shading his face from the hot burning sun, Eddie pulled his military cap down over his nose, and waited. Silence and fear slapped against their faith like the waves of the Pacific. Miraculously, Eddie felt something land on the top of his cap. It was a seagull! Rickenbacker would later describe how he sat perfectly still, planning his next move. He was handed an opportunity, but could he make it a miracle? Think about that sentence again. *He was handed an opportunity, but could he make it a miracle?* With the flash of his hands, he managed to grab the bird and subdue it. *Subdue is a nice way of saying to snap its little neck. Sad but necessary.* In no more a heroic way has a Seagull gone to its death than to provide life sustaining food for the men, and for some very needed bait for them to catch fish.

Rickenbacker had one chance to grab the bird. One. Many lives depended on it. He took the opportunity he was given and made it count. He made the shot! He scored the touchdown! He won the game! He took out the pigs! His well calculated, well played grab allowed the entire crew to remain alive at sea for twenty-four days. Was it a miracle or was it an opportunity well taken? I believe the bird was a miracle, the capture of it was a shot well taken.

In life we get many shots (opportunities, choices, and decisions). There are opportunities available any time night or day. Along with deciding which ones we are going to take comes the encouragement to make each one count. Here is a little secret they will not tell you in school. Are you ready to hear it? Your most important shots (opportunities, choices, decisions) will rarely identify themselves as your most important shots.

Let me explain. As I look back on my years of success in life and business, and my failures in the same, I have learned this great lesson. Are you ready to hear it? Okay ... here it is. The Big decisions often look like little decisions and then you wake up ten years later and find out that some of the decisions you made that seemed so insignificant at the time were actually the most significant, super-important, life or death decisions of your entire life. *FYI, I believe that last sentence may have been the longest grammatically correct sentence I have ever written.*

I am going to get very real with you. I will even name a topic. I say without a doubt that nobody would ever make the decision to have unprotected sex if they could look back on this decision from the future, realizing it was this particular sexual encounter where they contracted an STD or even an STI. Some might say, "But we don't have future vision glasses." True. Thus, we mortals must make every decision count. Every test is important because every little opportunity carries with it the possibility of being our big break or our big demise. Some matter little, some matter much, but you often cannot tell them apart until they are all over. That is why you must never let your guard down. Think. Postulate. Examine. Make every shot a shot with precision.

Sum It Up

As I look back on what I would call the most important decisions of my life, I did not know they were the most important ones until many years later. Rickenbacker knew the intense burden of his performance in bird catching, unfortunately most of us will not know how important our decisions are until after we make them. You may be asked to make a choice today. A choice is a decision. You may be asked to participate in an activity. An activity is a decision. You may be asked to buy something. A purchase is a decision. You may be told to think a certain way about an issue. Thoughts are the basis of all decisions. Choose today to make every decision count.

One Word: *Precision*

Action Point

What areas of your life are you flippantly going through as if it does not matter? What do you need to do about that?

#9 IT TURNS OUT THE PROBLEM WAS ME

Recognize your mistake patterns and deal with them...

My son turns to me and says, "Dad, you will never complete this level doing it that way!" C'mon! This is a bird game, a pig game. A bird and pig game on a phone screen. A free app. An eight year old can beat it. That's right, but the fifty year old was doing it all wrong, and doing it wrong persistently. My son told me to go for the farthest pig first, but there I sat trying to take out the closest pig first. He explained that I had to let the structure fall on the last pig in order for it to open up for me to "annihilate" (a word he loves) the closer pigs.

But I had already been doing it wrong for so long, I was stuck in a rut. I continued doing it my way. Until I finally gave up. When he got up to go to that little airplane bathroom, I tried it his way. He was right. Do not tell him I said that. *Insanity was once defined as doing the same thing over and over while expecting to achieve different results.* I had to recognize that I was doing it wrong in order to change to what needed to be done. *In case you are wondering, this is not another lesson about prioritizing.*

The greatest words I ever learnt to say were, "I was wrong." It is hard for a man to even get it out of his mouth. I think the first time I ever said it I choked as if there was a green pea caught in my windpipe. It was as though it caused an involuntary gag reflex. I could get out, "I was mistaken." That almost sounds like it was not my fault, but rather I was dubiously tricked into being wrong.

As I have matured I have come to believe that one of the greatest phrases ever created was, "I was wrong." It is a phrase that frees you to be ... well ... free! It frees you to be human.

I grew up in an era that somehow taught men that it was sissy to be wrong. A generation that somehow taught girls that it was somehow disempowering. I was taught that only losers were wrong! I have come to an understanding that that was a load of pig poop (pardon the game theme pun). There is a joy in being able to look another person in the face, man or woman or child and say, "I was wrong." In fact, I might go so far as to say that until you learn to master it you are not really a mature being.

Let's look for a minute at the ramifications of never being able to be wrong. When you are never wrong you can never learn. Learning requires saying one of two things. One, that I did not know that. Which in itself says I was wrong, even if it is just by lack of knowledge. Or two, that what I am learning is different from what I have been taught before, I was wrong in my prior knowledge. It is okay to be wrong. Without being wrong we could never move forward. Without being wrong, we would never have acquired the light bulb. We would still be trying to keep Bamboo sticks burning in Edison's bulbs. *Without the light bulb, every time we had a great idea, a candle would have to pop on in our brain. It is all connected.*

Let's try an exercise together. Say, out loud, "I am wrong." I know you're not wrong but just pretend. Win an at-home Oscar for your acting like you are wrong. Say it again louder, "I am wrong." Oh that was beautiful. Isn't it so liberating to be mature enough to be wrong. The word often used for being wrong is the word repent. To repent is to understand where we were wrong, verbalize it, and do our best to alter our course to become right from that point on.

Sum It Up

When we are mature enough to admit our mistakes we can stop the "insanity" (remember the definition) of our lives and get onto a proper course. What course are you on that you have been refusing to try a different way? What is your case for insanity? What dead horse are you strapped to trying to get to the rodeo? Think about it.

One Word: *Repent*

Action Point

Can you make a mental list of the things you have been wrong about in the past? Are there any things in your mind or heart that you know you are wrong about now but somehow to immature to admit it? It takes a big man or woman to repent. Be big!

#10 ACTIONS SPEAK LOUDER THAN MEGAPHONES

There's a reason it's called 'Show & Tell' not 'Tell and Show'…

Well, he asked. As soon as he arrived back from the bathroom, "Did you complete that level? How'd you do it?" I could have lied. I could have said, "My extreme patience paid off. I overcame it with sheer wit and wisdom garnered from nothing but the very genes coursing through my enlightened body." I didn't. I swallowed the green peas hard, and said, "I was wrong, I had to go back and do it your way."

This invoked my son to a small celebration, followed by an "in your seat victory dance", followed by a round of high-fives and three extremely loud "WHO'S THE MAN?" chants. It was over the top. *I am told this type of action once got angels kicked out of heaven.* My then very proud son launched into a systematic approach in telling me how his bird launch prowess for every level after that. Well, he did that until I reached a limit. To which I nicely asked him to shut the hole whereby he consumes pie. Please understand that his mother does not like us to use the phrase, "Shut up." Thus we try to find other creative ways to say the same thing. I think it makes the gesture more palatable. She does not. *She also hates our lines about welding your bicuspids together, licking some crazy glue, and of course the age old… having your mouth surgically and irreversibly removed.*

Here is our lesson for today friends. Nobody likes a braggart. Nobody likes those people who are *always* right. Those people who start every sentence with, "Well I'll tell you what you ought to do!" As if they are the supreme source of world knowledge. Now this might sound a bit hypocritical coming from someone who is writing a book about wisdom. Please hear me out. The wisdom I am sharing with you was not written by me. I take no credit for it. Great teachers and mentors have passed this along to me, I am just transcribing the short version of it. But let's get back to the point. The greatest way you can ever give advice to another is to show them how you are doing it right in action, not in bragging advertisement. In other words, close your meat muncher (there's another one) and let them see your success. Make yourself available to them and let them ask you for the secrets to your greatness. Pardon the sarcasm my friends.

A quote, often attributed to Francis of Assisi, reads "Share your good message ... and sometimes use words." With a little research you find that this quote is actually a paraphrase of some of his writings and certainly his life. Nevertheless, it is good truth whether it is a paraphrase or not. I know a basketball coach that does not let the second string players participate in real games until he hears them stop their critical attitude toward the players that are first string. Some might say that trash talk (telling someone how bad they are and how good you are) is acceptable in sports. I prefer a person to show me how good they are by their skills and possess the personal confidence to be genuinely nice after they beat me 21 to 0. Now we have someone who can beat me and receive my respect.

My oldest son has a favorite basketball player, LeBron James. He also has a least favorite basketball player, Kobe Bryant. I have informed him that they are both amazingly gifted players, to which he agrees. His argument is that his least favorite aforementioned player is just too stuck on himself. He is great ... and he knows it ... and he is ready to share with everyone his so-called superior skills. Who do you know that is always telling others how great they are? Is it ever you?

Sum It Up

Actions speak louder than words. Show first - tell later. Have you ever become caught in the braggart trap? Do you know someone who is real good at telling everyone how great they are? Don't point! I am just asking. You are no different if you act the same way.

One Word: *Example*

Action Point

Spend a day without ever speaking a word negatively about anything or anyone. The next day do not speak a word of how awesome you are. The very next day do both of those simultaneously. And smile while you're at it. You look great when you smile!

#11 REVENGE ON THE PIGS

Don't destroy your future seeking revenge for the past...

Do you like the white bird? The giant chicken looking avian who seeks to destroy the pigs by dropping eggs on them. Let's look at the logic for a moment. This pre-pubescent brain child of a bird is seeking vengeance on pigs for what reason? They have stolen her eggs. Thus, to seek revenge she is now throwing more eggs at them. How does that make any sense. As my Uncle Dan used to say, "You can't fix stupid!" *Of course he would say it with a cigarette hanging out of his unemployed mouth. So we never really paid him that much attention anyway. Yes, everybody has an Uncle like that somewhere.*

I have always felt that there was a underlying problem with this Angry Bird game. Not a code problem. Not a graphics problem. Those are spectacular. The problem is the logic flaw of the story line. I am not saying the game wasn't brilliantly designed, for it is. I am not saying it is not clever, intriguing, addictive, entertaining, challenging, and a number of other adjectives I could toss into the mix. I just believe that at the root there is a horrible flaw in the birds purpose, with all due respect to the game. Stay with me here. According to those who write articles about the game and the game itself, winning is achieved by exacting revenge on the pigs for stealing bird eggs.

I have to be honest, I have a real problem with that. I have grown up watching the middle east being torn up over people who have been seeking revenge on each other for decades. No good has ever come of it. There revenge has seemingly only produced more angry birds and more angry pigs. Anger begets anger and revenge begets revenge. It is reciprocal!

I love the History Channel. Daily this channel serves up to my HD converter box American Restoration, Storage Wars, Ice Road Truckers, Pawn Stars, Swamp People, and so much more. I give them five stars and two thumbs up! When it comes to television, I also love investigative reporting of all kinds. Recently I watched a short documentary about an ongoing family feud between the Hatfield family and the McCoy family. This hillbilly mountain family war has reached iconoclastic levels. Two families started fighting over one thing and carried out a vengeance spree that killed far too many of each family for many years. Fighting over a past injustice almost wiped out their entire families.

I am fighting the desire to tell you that after seeing the character of these long term moronic vengeance takers, I can't help but think that the elimination of their entire gene pool would almost certainly have been welcomed by a peace loving society. Some uncivilized societies have taught their children that if someone takes your eggs, then you should go and take their eggs. I think if you take my eggs once, shame on you, I will build a bigger defense system. I will guard my future eggs with guards. I will learn from the injustice that someone did to me and turn it into a learning experience. I will not spend the rest of my life trying to exact revenge.

Some have wasted their entire lives trying to seek revenge instead of living the remainder of their life in educated security. They call it living and "an eye for an eye and a tooth for a tooth". People who live by that adage will end up blind and toothless. They may also die by it.

There was an actual cartoon about this Hatfield and McCoy feud when I was a kid. I watched it. It taught me that it was fun and even funny to get back at your neighbor for everything they did that you felt was disturbing to you. Well at least that was the surface lesson of each episode. After lengthy viewing, the smarter children (I was not in that group), and those who possessed a triple digit I.Q's, realized that these people wasted their lives fighting for nothing. Many of my generation wonder if some of the wars that have taken tens of thousands of lives of our young men and women, could have been far better fought by the construction of fences rather than invasions.

Don't ask me, I want to stay out of politics. Ask those of your generation who lost their father or mother in a war. Ask them if they think the purpose or outcome was worth that parent's life.

This chapter is not political! This chapter is an intervention of clear thought. A reminder that revenge only causes more revenge. The larger, brighter person has to move on to the future and not live in the past actions of another. All of us have had tragedy come our way from the cause of another. What will we do with it? Will we spend our lives blowing our own children up to destroy the evil doers, or will we refuse to allow them to steal our futures? In real life, birds were made to fly.

Sum It Up

When a bird stops flying (as it was made to do) and let's itself be sidelined by anger and revenge, it is a tragic waste of bird potential. Don't ever let yourself become a flightless - futureless tool because of your own vengeance or the tool of someone else's vengeance. I believe that you were born to fly ... so fly! Vengeance is like drinking poison in hopes that someone else will die. I guess you can't fix stupid. But I'm hoping you are not stupid!

One Word: *Response*

Action Point

Is there someone you spend your time plotting against? Is there a name so powerful in your psyche that every time it is heard you start devising plans for their demise? Move on. Just move on.

#12 IF AT FIRST YOU DON'T SUCCEED, TRY, TRY AGAIN

I love the start over tab...

I love this game! I feel like I am playing it a little too much right now but I will call my indulgence, research for this book. I like the fact that on each level if I don't win I can start over. If I fail, I can go back and try again. The ability to try again is a good thing. My life has been filled with great successes on the second, third, and forty-third "try again"! I am glad that this game allows me second chances. My Dad used to say, "Repetition is the best teacher!" *It had to be better than my third grade teacher Mrs. Harper.*

I believe that life is divided into a few different categories. First, there are opportunities that only come once in a lifetime. Fortunately these comprise of only a small percentage of our daily lives. Secondly, there are opportunities that will repeat themselves, and tests that must be completed in order to achieve a new level of humanity and personal growth. The beautiful thought is that ninety-nine percent of life's opportunities are repetitive options. You can do them over! Celebrate! You will get another shot! Finally, you have those unnecessary time wasting opportunities that attempt to distract us from doing something great. It is to be hoped that you will not spend your life in the unnecessary time waster section of life. You only have one life, make it count for something great.

But again, as for that second section, you will get a number of opportunities to get them right. You will get a do over. Take the do-overs. Take the start again. Whatever you do, don't rush the learning process of life. Take as many do overs as your life will give you. Play each time with greater skill and greater knowledge from past victories and past defeats. Use your amazing mind to devise new and better ways to compete on every level you are called to play. Again, in life not every level offers us the ability to go back and play again. Rejoice in the getting a start over on the ones you can.

Sometimes in life you start out headed in one direction and then realize the path you are on is one of those unnecessary time wasters. You realize it is a futureless path. You need to go back and start again quickly. Sometimes it takes making new friends that will encourage you in the path you really want to go. Sometimes it is a big move to another location that will be required for your success. Just get busy at starting again.

So if you would say to me that right now in your life you are failing in an area, stop! Go back to square one. Come at your problem or situation from a new approach. Get back to the basics and learn the core requirements to complete the level you are trying to achieve.

I breezed through high school on a Business English track. I was not going to go to college for I was going to start my own business. I was going to be counting big money and wearing lots of bling when my college bound friends were still trying to pass their college entrance exams. *I would be raking in the green while my other friends were still learning how to pronounce Greek words. Ha Ha Ha!*

Little did I know that my business plan would fall flat and I would wind up in college myself. My college start was rocky. The only way I could succeed in college was to go back and start again. I had to take precollege courses to be able to complete the harder courses. My creative writing teacher loved my creative stories, she just kept asking where I learned my English grammar, and when I was going to learn how to spell. I joke not. I took pre-college algebra twice. Finally, however, I was prepared enough to go forward with victory.

Sum It Up

When you find yourself up against an obstacle that you cannot seem to beat, go back and start again. If you can, go back and find out what you need to know to tackle your problem again. And again. And again if need be. It is in doing things over and over that we become a master of them. Practice repeatedly winning.

One Word: *Repetition*

Action Point

Take something to day that you already do. An instrument, a sport, a hobby, a school class. Do it again. Can you recite your multiplication tables? Do it again and again until you can do them backwards. Now you are master multiplicator. *I don't think that multiplicator is really a word, but you know what I mean.*

#13 WHICH BIRD ARE YOU?

Birds of a feather flock together...

I like the big fat red angry bird. I don't even know his name. I like his moves! *His skills are off the chain (or hook, I forget which one it is supposed to be). If I were an Angry Bird I would want to be that one.* Plus it would get my picture on the front of this book and T-shirts everywhere. Can you name all the birds in an Angry Bird line up on all the games? If you can, you are good, very good. *At my age, I do well to remember the names of all aunts, uncles, and cousins. Most of them I just call "Cuz." The only time I see them is at weddings, funerals, and the occasional Christmas party. "Hey Cuz.". "Good to see you, Cuz.". Now get away from me be-cuz I can't even remember your name.*

Let's talk about identification for a minute. Do you have a favorite bird? Do you secretly wish they all exploded? Do you wish they all divided into three birds when you tapped the screen? Do you wish that they would fly over and poop on the windshields of the pigs first to make them squeal with anger? We all do, it's natural.

If you could teleport yourself into the game, which bird would you teleport into? Who do you mostly identify with? In life we are often most influenced by the company we keep. Yes, our friends will determine who we will become and we will determine who they will become. So we have two great responsibilities. We have the responsibility to be the best person we can be, this will help others reach their full potential. Then we have the responsibility to hang out with those who will build us up and not tear us down.

Who are your friends? Most people think that a friend is someone who just happens to be near you of similar age. That person is simply a bystander, a proximity sharer. A true friend is someone who is always trying to encourage you and push you to do better. A friend is someone who desires the best for you and wants you to succeed as much as they succeed. A real friend is generous, caring, sharing, and a prized possession. A genuine friend is hard to find. They are rarer than large diamonds. They are those who chose to walk through life with you in good times and bad times. They will not use you or abuse you. A friend is an influencer!

Unfortunately many bystanders (enemies) come to you secretly disguised as friends. For the sake of our illustration we could call them pigs dressed in birds clothing! Be careful to determine what you have in front of you before you welcome this person to be a "friend" in your life. The person in front of you may be the biggest and craftiest pig at the party. Your success in life will be greatly influenced by the company (friends) you keep. It is better to wait for a real friend than to be hand in hand with a scorpion.

Sum It Up

People say that we are known by the company we keep. Birds of a feather flock together. That is a rhyming way of saying that if you hang out with bad people you become a bad person. If you hang out with good people you will become a good person. Hang out with negative people and you become negative. You see a pattern here? And those watching you will know you by knowing any of the people you allow to be in your inner circle. Choose your friends wisely. It is better to have no friends, than to have friends who are not really being a friend to you.

One Word: *Associates*

Action Point

Make a list of the people you hang with. Do they build you up or tear you down? Who needs to come of the associates list?

#14 TURN YOUR DEVICE UPSIDE DOWN

Change your perspective and see a whole new game...

Do you know how to tie a knot? How many different knots can you tie? How many different knots can you untie. The city of Gordium was famous during the Classical period for possessing the legendary Gordian Knot. It was quite a knot. It was a massive twist of loops and turns and every twist of the rope seemed to cover up any hint of how the knot could be solved. Local fame of the knot brought many wise men to match their intellect against the knot. Many failed. A prophecy held that whoever was able to untie this mess of twisted rope would become King of Asia. Many men tried, but all failed. Then one day a young Macedonian man rode into the city. He looked carefully at the famed knot, unsheathed his sword and sliced it in two. *Knot puzzle solved!* Today, we remember that young man as Alexander the Great.

Perspective is a good word. When I say that word, does it mean anything to you? In the game it can be the size of which I view the playing field. It is the zooming in for a better look at the structure of the bunker so that one might better decide how to attack the problem.

It is also stepping back from the close up so that one could better aim the birds at the exact place where one had decided would be the best place to hit for most destruction. Perspective! I have to admit that at times I turned the game upside down and played it from a different angle to overcome a level. That can be perspective also. I learned that, playing another great app called Un-Block Me. The other day I purposely played Angry Birds Rio with my device completely upside down. It must be similar to playing in Australia. Try it! It was awesome. *I double-dawg dare you!* It was like playing a whole new game, and this time gravity was dyslexic.

One of my favorite movies has always been Dead Poet Society. Robin Williams plays the role of a teacher attempting to teach a group of young men about life and it's true journey. For one exercise, Robin (the actual character's name I don't remember) asks all the boys to walk to the front of the class and stand on his big desk. They are being asked to see the room from a fresh perspective, a new point of view. His point is that we can better understand every situation if we can view it from many angles. He taught them that what looks one way from the student's chair looks very different perched on top the teacher's desk. His lesson was that problems can often be solved when we observe them from different observation points.

The pigs know the weak spots in their bunkers. So get inside the pigs head and think of what that might be. This will make you a better chess player. This will make you a well-paid asset to any business you go into.

Sum It Up

To be successful in Angry Birds you have to examine the pig bunkers, and even watch the effects of gravity on your bird. Sometimes the unconventional way will work for you when the normal way does not. Some days you need to get in there and take the time to untie the knots in your world, and other days you need to cut the ties with a sword and go on to greater things like Alexander the Great.

One Word: *Perspective*

Action Point

Is there an obstacle you are facing? Maybe it is a disagreement with your parents or even a friend. Look at the situation from a different angle. Put yourself in their shoes. Pretend you are them and try to see it from their angle. Then put yourself in the mind of others around you. Get a new look. Get perspective.

.

#15 CHEAT CODES

Easier ways to win at the game of life...

As of the writing of this book there are no legitimate cheat codes listed in any google search. Upon checking with my son, who I am sure has scoured the internet for anything that would help him gain a higher score, there appears to be none offered. The sites that brag about cheat codes are just giving advice on how to play it. Some sites have other players telling you how they beat the game. Apparently there is no sequence of buttons to push to win each level with little effort. *In my estimation it would be a very boring game if it were that easy, I would have to go back to taking candy from babies or tipping cows.*

This cheat code *phenomenon* is interesting to me. In a world where we all hate a cheater. In a world where we strip world class awards from those who are caught using performance enhancing drugs, we seem to have no problem personally using cheat codes for any games we play. The world recently watched a world renowned bicyclist be disgraced and destroyed for cheating. My generation saw it in baseball betting scandals and even politics. Nevertheless, we keep on googling "cheat codes" for everything.

The word I would like to introduce is - ethics. It is a deep word, it has heavy meaning. It is the code by which a society or group choses to live. Some refer to situational ethics, believing that our actions can vary depending upon the dilemma we are faced with. For example, some might say that stealing is wrong, unless it is something that you really - really want.

In your world one might believe that our best friend would not steal our girlfriend or boyfriend from us. We would say that is not ethical. Breaking that would be to have a friend that did not have integrity! We all have a set of ethics. It varies from person to person what they consider ethical, moral, or right. You live in a world that has chosen to make universal ethics a thing of the past, but nevertheless, people still appreciate when people treat them right.

You might have heard about the "Golden Rule" when you were a child. In its simplest form, it pushes us to treat everyone the way we would like to be treated. Some people call it integrity. It's based on fair and balanced justice for all. It proclaims equal rights for all parties. That means that one person doesn't get to use cheat codes or have special privileges that the other person doesn't have either. Depending on which person you are in the matter probably determines where you stand on the matter. People of wealth or power often think that they are the only ones deserving of special privileges. Unfortunately we all fall into that trap at times. Do you have integrity? Can you be trusted?

On a side note, let me give you a great legal, moral, and ethical cheat code for life. It is a universally ethical cheat code because it is available to everyone. It is known as education. Education? Yes! Education is the shortcut to a push forward. That is not to say that educated people don't need to work hard to succeed. No way! But education is definitely a boost in apartment size and whether or not your room has a view of the lake or the parking lot.

But let's get back on topic. A person of universal integrity (honest level justice for everyone including themselves) is a person whom others like to do business with. They are a person whom others like to make contracts with. They are the ones who are trusted with the best relationships, and thus share in the joys of that goodness.

There are two ways you can live your life: with ethics or without ethics. One will lead to being respected and the other will lead to disrespect. Those lacking ethics most often find themselves surrounded with other lacking good ethics in a jail cell.

Sum It Up
Set quality "Golden Rule" standards by which you will live, and live by them. Don't alter your integrity for any reason. Choose to make those unbreakable! When you treat others the same way that you wish to be treated you will find that to be a propulsion forward in your life, family, and career. Let your name be the one mentioned when others name an ethical person.

One Word: *Integrity*

Action Point
Are you treating everyone in your world with the same honesty? Are you a person of justice or inequality? What would you have to do to make the word integrity become repeatedly mentioned on your Wikipedia page?

#16 BUT WAIT, THERE'S MORE!

The free edition cost me plenty...

Have you ever downloaded an app that really stunk? One of those that you were sorry you wasted the twenty-seconds it took to download it? It looked so good in the description! Furthermore it was FREE! Of course there were those online nay-sayers who rated it pathetically as one star. They must all be wrong. Certainly it will be most excellent, there is one guy who gave it almost two and a half stars. Come on, you know the app I am talking about. Maybe it was the one that crashed and locked up your new iPhone? *I don't know ... I am only suggesting.*

You need to choose what is worth doing with your life. We are all lacking maturity from time to time. But in those rare seconds of clear thought we need to decide what we want to spend our life playing. This is not just for games, it is for habits, spouses, relationships, jobs, and the list goes on.

Success in life will be determined by what you chose to spend your life doing. I was about thirteen years old when I snubbed the naysayers and put a cigarette into my mouth. What did they know. Look at all the cool people who were doing it. Just because a few medical professionals said it would kill you (crash your device) I puffed on. As a thirteen year old, you can't just sit in your living room puffing away as your parents comment on what a fine brand you smoke. Thus I did what all my other, not so brilliant friends who bought into this game did. I hid.

While others were playing baseball, football, and running track, I was seeing how many hits I could get off a cancer stick behind the bleachers and washing my hands with gasoline (another toxin by the way) to kill the smell. I must have smelled worse than a BP Oil employee.

When you are thirteen it is hard to convince your parents that you always smell like smoke from going into a convenience store, if you get my drift (no pun intended). For the next five years I hid out with the others who also bought into an App that stunk. Literally! And now that I am older I am watching the results of that App in many of those friends, maybe even myself. Now that I am older I mourn the loss of those years I spent thinking I was cool when I was the one being smoked. Do you know what I mean?

But this life lesson is not about smoking, it is about choosing. Choosing wisely where and how we want to spend our life. Career decisions are life apps. Dating decisions are life apps. Habit decisions are life Apps. Dining decisions are life Apps. Study decisions are life Apps. What game would you like to play for the rest of your life? Don't know? Would it be smart to do a little research on the future of the game you are playing? I think so. Choose wisely!

Truth be known, every free app you download is genuinely vying to get you to buy the non-free version of it. Every product you see advertised is built around trying to get you to get more. Everything in life is urging you to consume more of it. By nature, that is how it works. That is how businesses succeed, how app designers make money, it is how the free-market revolves. Understand that. This is why people say there are no free lunches. People rarely give you anything without wanting something, little or big, in return. Any free lunch that does not come from your mother probably comes with an associated request for something in return. *Maybe even your mother's lunch from time to time.*

I remember my dear High School Professor Crandall Miller. I think he must have been a hundred years old when he taught my eleventh grade class. To say he was what we considered narrow minded goes without saying. He had a saying that he must have said every day at least twice. He said, "What you feed grows... what you starve dies...you never satisfy anything by feeding it...you only increase its appetite." *What?* Let me put it into wisdom we can more easily understand, for I didn't quite understand the old man back then either. Years removed, I now do. When you stuff your belly with potato chips your stomach will expand and insanely demand more potato chips. It will continue to do this until you explode. If you let it. The only way to stop the expansive ravenous rampage is to stop feeding your stomach potato chips. *Deny the Ruffles! Smash the bag!*

When you download a free App, the App makers desire you to love it so much that you can't put it down! They would love it if you were hooked on it like a drug. Hooked on it, you will quickly need to upgrade to the better, more costly, version. Cha-ching! ... $$$ ... Stock Market wins! Then they continue to sell you more "app-iness" (electronic cessation thumb tapping happiness) in small downloadable doses ad infinitum. *Forever! Hooked like a fish!*

Be careful what you feed your mind. Anything we feed to our mind becomes a possible controller of that mind. Whether that be Apps, drugs, culture, politics, or even ideas. The more we feed it the more our appetite grows for more of the same. It can be dangerous. Just like my childhood smoking. I started smoking cigarettes, then the cigarettes started smoking me. I had to have them. It was no longer the delicious flavor of burnt tar, poison carcinogenic, stained finger, and the delightful truck stop bathroom-like aroma of nicotine, I needed the cancer sticks so that I wouldn't shake. *They tell me about 300,000 people died last year from that bad app. We will most likely lose the same amount this year.* Long term happiness is determined by the game you choose to play.

Sum It Up

What you consume is what your body and mind will grow to crave. You must, therefore, determine what is worthy of risking consumption. If success is really being happy with what you get one must choose wisely what they chase after.

One Word: *Appetite*

Action Point

Be careful what you download to your game system, or to your body. Got any apps you need to delete?

#17 SELECTIVE MEMORIES

Memories, how we forget them...

So today I found myself on another flight to another city. It was too short to sleep, although that has never stopped me during a boring lecture. *Not even in the boring lectures I was giving.* So I pulled out my iPhone and plopped my fat little finger down on the Angry Birds game again. Hey, if you are going to write about them you better know and understand them. I am just saying, "Respect the bird!" It is just that simple. I have to admit that I was a little rusty as I had forsaken my responsibility to master the birds due to my incredibly taxing schedule. Sure I had lots of commuting time, but the State Police take a dim view of people playing with Apps while driving on the interstate. *I know that now! "Look officer. Sure, I smashed the guard rail, but I think there might have been pigs under there ... I'm just saying." However, I have progressive insurance and it is all better now. Pigs can drive!*

So I sat this morning reacquainting myself with which birds do what. First we have the good old red bird. This bird goes where it is launched, no special gimmicks, just good old faithful. Then you have the cute little blue bird that splits into three smaller birds when you tap it while still in flight. This bird I call the MPD bird. Then you have the yellow cone headed bird that will increase its velocity when tapped in air. This increased speed allows it to deliver greater damage to the pig bunkers. There is that green/orange Toucan breakfast cereal looking fowl that operates like a boomerang to slip up on the pigs blind side and wallop them. Then we have what appears to be a white egg-laying chicken who drops egg bombs on the pigs. Again, I don't understand why we are using eggs to seek vengeance on the pigs for stealing our eggs. *Remember Uncle Danny said, "You can't fix stupid." It is what it is.* Then there is the granddaddy Bird Warrior of them all ... the BIG RED BIRD. *This is a flying steam roller for you baby ... A churning urn of burning funk!*

I took the trip down memory lane because if I am going to jump back into the game at a high level I need to remember who does what, when they do that best, and how to make them do it. Did that make any sense? Let me put it another way. *I needed to remember how to shoot a bird effectively.*

A memory is one of the most important things you can ever use. Most of the times we fail at accomplishing a task, even a repetitive task, is because we were either not paying attention to what we were doing, or simply forgot how to do the task. I remember dear old Coach Goldberg, back in sixth grade. *He used to keep his gym shorts so high up on his belly you could see the Rabbi's initials on his circumcision. Ouch!* Nevertheless, he was a good coach and history teacher. He always said, every day, multiple times, over and over, "Those who cannot remember the past are forced to repeat it." Now as kids we all thought he meant that if we can't remember our history homework that we would have to take the class again. It was not until I got older that I realized he was talking about life.

If I am going to win at angry birds I am going to have to remember all that I know about the game and the birds and the pigs and their bunkers. Then I will be able to play with success. Playing with success in life is partially due to remembering the victories and the mistakes of the past. Remembering how the other teammates play. By all means you need to recognize similar game set-ups to overcome similar challenges. The old adage, History repeats itself, is true. So we must remember the past. Hindsight being 20/20 becomes the building blocks for our future success.

Sum It Up

When you can clearly remember how you won a victory in the past, it is easier to win a similar victory in the present. If you can't remember your past mistakes you will have to experience them repeatedly. How foolish is that?

One Word: *Remember*

Action Point

What are you failing at that you failed at before? What do you need to remember to overcome that hurdle next time you face it? Think a while. Sit and think a while. Remember.

#18 DON'T GIVE UP

It isn't over until the battery is dead...

I'm sure that by now you have played the game as much as I have. You have squealed with delight over the destruction of the pigs. Although squealing seems like the wrong sound to make over the demise of pigs. Squealing is more of a pig celebration sound. Big deal, chirping is so hard to do! If you do chirp in public they will take you away to see a special kind of doctor. *That is, unless you are chirping in Wal-Mart, then you would simply be blending in. But I digress.*

This game is rather addictive. You start playing and you just don't want to stop. That's not so bad. Wanting to fight until your enemy is completely defeated sure beats laying down and having the enemy climb over the walls and wake you with the point of a sword. As a parent I worry about my children playing video games until they pass out on the floor or until the battery dies. Nonetheless, as a parent I am encouraged to see that there are still some things that excite my kids enough for them to play until they drop. I am encouraged to see passion almost anywhere in a passionless generation.

A great author of years past said, "The battle is not given to the strong, nor the race given to the swift. Victory is given to the one who endures to the end." So it is with your bird adventure. You have learned that you can arrive at new levels if you work hard enough to get there. You have learned that when you add time and experience together it pays off. That is a great lesson to learn in life. We are in an age of quitters. You are growing up in an age where everyone gives up soon as it becomes difficult. I'm so sorry about that. I'm sorry that my generation taught you by our bad example to run from anything that is not easy or fun. Many of you will face financial crisis in our national economy because of that. I apologize.

Just because we taught you by our bad example though, does not mean that you are required to continue. Use your right as the next generation to change our bad ways. Rebel against our apathy and rise to action. Never give up. I believe it was the great Prime Minister of England, Winston Churchill, who, during the time of WWII, spoke these famous words to a group of school students, "Never give in. Never give in. Never, never, never, never—in nothing, great or small, large or petty—never give in. Never yield to force. Never yield to the apparently overwhelming might of the enemy."

Sum It Up

Anyone can be lazy. Anyone can be a quitter. Winners do not quit. Winners play the game until their legs won't hold them up anymore. Then, they only rest to regain their energy to get back in the game. They possess stamina! Your success in life will be based upon your ability to get in there and fight until the end. Stamina! High school will not be easy, but you can finish it. Stamina! Attaining good grades will not be easy but you can receive them if you work hard enough. Stamina! Completing college can be a bear, but it is a bear that you can take down with your determination and stamina.

One Word: *Stamina*

Action Point

Find something worth doing and do it until you drop. Then get up and do it some more. Prove to yourself that you are a bigger person than others thought you were. Prove to yourself that you are a bigger person than maybe even you thought you were.

#19 GAME OVER

All games come to an end...

Back in the day, long before video games, when the West was young, and two guns beat four aces, in the age known as BC (Before Cable TV), way back when, before computers, and iPods. Back when iWatches, Google Glasses, and gyro free standing motorcycles were simply rumors, we played different games. We played games such as Chop-the-Tree, in order to get enough fire wood so we wouldn't freeze to death. We played Milk-The-Cow, so that we would have something to drink with our oatmeal. We played Plow-The-Field, to get vegetables for our family to eat for lunch. They were good games but not nearly as thumb inspiring as Angry Birds. But fun and obviously life sustaining nonetheless.

I was going to be one of those people who got through their entire life without being a *gamer guy.* Now I am sure that most of you would not call me a one, since the only game I really play is this crazy bird game, right? Let me let you in on a secret. I also found a game called Fruit Ninja! Crazy! I love it! *Even though I never wanted to be a professional ninja I am sure that if I had, I would have been acting out my aggression on some evil empire and not on some albeit fresh ... vertically flying fruit.* Whatever! I have since become a chopping champion. Who doesn't like the sound of that sword swishing through the air?

From that game I learned that if you get overly knife happy you will end up chopping the wrong stuff and blow yourself up. Not good! Patience grasshopper, patience (ask your grandfather to explain the grasshopper reference to you).

As mentioned previously I also found a game called UnBlock Me. There are several variations of this, but in all of them you have to get one block out of the puzzle by moving the other blocks around. You face a few block walls both mentally and visually in your quest for block freedom. With continued perseverance you eventually maneuver correctly and find the escape method. This escape is met with a wonderful musical finale that I would just love to have played every-time I complete any task in my real life, so glorious it is. This game taught me that you can get where you need to go, or want to go, by helping others get to where they need to go. Teamwork works!

These video games have taught me that they are, in themselves rather addictive in nature. You want to play them. They offer excitement and challenge. We like excitement and challenge. I remember my mom used to yell out the window, "You're not gonna be laughing when somebody gets hurt!" Mom was wrong. If someone got hurt, we all laughed. It was the price of really good hard play. We took the risk because of the excitement and challenge. Life is a challenge and we take the risks and run the race because of the possible reward of the victor.

Like the video games, life is addictive! You want to play it! You want to enjoy it. You want to live it. Sure there may be times when you get discouraged, but you were born to live. Just like our Angry Bird game, life will bring you great challenges, but also like our Angry Bird game we learn to be victorious through the obstacles we overcome.

Within life there are sub games if I can call them that. Like Angry Birds has Space, and Rio, and who knows how many more will arrive on my iPad? Life has amazing chapters that will consume your time for a season upon season.

Those times will be occupations that you will have, friends that you will share time with, relationships, and marriage. Marriage ... now that is a biggie! There will be bills you will have to pay that may seem to take a lifetime. Those are often the debtor games that you create for yourself trying to find more games. *Some people call these credit cards. Ouch!* Don't forget the schools you will have to graduate from.

There will be many lessons you will have to learn along your journey. There will be no skipping ahead. There will be those episodes of life that will repeat themselves until you become the victor of them or they become the victor of you. *My little hint ... don't stinkin' lose.*

If I may add one little point of wisdom here. In this game of life, don't mistake movement for success. Simply being busy is not something to be attained. Being busy without accomplishment only brings frustration without payoff. Personally in the daily episodes of my life, I want to see the completion of each task and a greater knowledge at the end of each day. I want to know that I gave each responsibility the best I could give. I want to know in my own mind that I faced each challenge with all my energy. I want to know inside of myself that I was not a quitter, or lazy, or a cheater. I want to make each day of my life a victory for my own personal integrity and that of my children. I don't want to be sidetracked, and I don't want to become addicted to failure.

Responsibility are episodes you will have more of as you get older. Let's remember that the word responsibility is taken from two words. The first is *response*. It is our following action to a need, an idea, or even a dream.

The second word is *ability*. The second word is not disability! It is ability. The word itself says that we have what it takes to complete the task and win the game. Responsibility is given to those whom others believe in enough to give them the responsibility. When you receive responsibilities it means those around you believe in you and believe you are mature enough to handle them. Wear "responsibilities" as a badge of honor! *Celebrate maturity.*

I don't buy a lot of art. I did once, then I sold it. *You can only have so much Thomas Kinkade before you snap and start shouting out incoherencies at a live magic show in Vegas!* I do have a framed Angry Birds T-shirt that my children bought me at the airport. It is framed because it is two sizes too small for me to wear, so now it is a poster. Cotton art! I have another motivational art poster. If Sharpie Marker calligraphy on cardboard is still considered art, the last remaining art I own is one of those motivational poems. My handmade poster says, and I will paraphrase for brevity:

Today is a day given to us to use as we see fit.
We can use it for gain or loss.
We can use it for good or evil.
We must be very aware of this one thing...
Whatever we do with today,
We are exchanging for one day of our life.
Yes, we trade one day of our precious life,
For our achievements today.
Trade it for gain not loss.
Trade it for good not evil.
Trade it for kindness and not hatred.
Make the most of it. Experience victory.
Give it the best effort.
So that we will not look back...
Regretting the price we paid for it.

Sum It Up

All games come to an end. Make sure that the life you lived was worth the time and resources your life consumed. Make sure that you did something worthy of the time you received. Don't settle for less than the full potential of you. You are amazing! At least you have that potential. Live for something worth dying for so that you might inspire the next generation. Live for something worth dying for so that you might be able to close your eyes at peace with yourself and your Creator.

One Word: *Live*

Action Point

Learn from your time with the Angry Birds. Move forward. Live successfully! Live large! Live big! Live fantastically! Live.

Made in the USA
Charleston, SC
09 May 2014